The Magnificent Miracle

Jarrett Nathan Klein

ISBN: 1500717274
ISBN 13: 9781500717278
Library of Congress Control Number: 2014913981
Createspace Independent Publishing Platform
North Charleston, SC

Dedicated to the children of the world.

In the near future a magnificent miracle will happen. With the help of a wise wizard, a caring unicorn will enter upon a magnificent miracle. Together they will change history. Read on to find out what happens when Imagination and reality are combined.

Once upon a time there lived a unicorn
in the land of Unizard. Her name was Chime. The
one thing Chime desired most was
a horn, for she had never grown one.

One wintery night, a wizard appeared.
He said he would grant Chime whatever
she desired. So he gave her a horn and he
also wanted her to travel on a long journey
to understand and learn what was
happening around the world.

She wandered upon a campsite. There were cannons piled along the riverbank.

Toward the evening, Chime heard the cannons conversing with each other about how they do not want to be a part of this violent behavior.

That night, she heard the blasts of shooting guns and peered in that direction. Standing before her, four men dressed in black clothing were practicing shooting for the ongoing war they were involved in. She felt saddened.

A few days later she awoke at a schoolyard.
She witnessed a terrible sight of kids
being shot. The sadness around Chime
made her think about how terrible
and violent the world can be.

Now she came upon country after country witnessing acts of violence involving guns. Again, she felt sad.

And so on ... and so on ... she felt sad.

Because of these atrocities, Chime began to cry and could not believe how it feels to lose the ones you love the most.

Chime awoke to the sound of running water and before her stood a mighty castle.

As she crossed the moat, the doors
slowly began to open.

Suddenly, the wizard she knew many
moons ago appeared. And with a spark of
his magic wand, he empowered the unicorn's horn
to burst into millions of particles.

And every one of those pieces traveled
long distances around the world, to find
the guns and the cannons... and if that magical
particle touched either a gun or a cannon,
they would never function again.

So this is the magical tale of the magnificent miracle that happened with the help of a wise wizard and a caring unicorn named Chime.

When Jarrett Klein wrote this book,
he was a ten-year old fourth grade student
at Ojus Elementary School. He was born on
November 28, 1989 in North Miami Beach,
Florida. His hobbies include playing basketball
and writing creative books. That is why he chose
to write another magnificent book.